The Nature of Things
Grand Canyon

The Nature of Things
Grand Canyon

Poetic Reveries - Volume One

by Bruce Hibma

Published by Bruce R. Hibma
3814 Voltaire Avenue
Raleigh, TN 38128

ISBN: 978-1-304-49378-1

brucieh@bellsouth.net

Cover Design: Rick Hoover

To My wife Joanne
and to those with ears to hear

The Nature of Things

This poem came out of my wonderment of all creation. Thinking of the amount of time gone by and the time mankind is able to be on the earth. There seems to be only a short time here where everything is exactly right for our existence. This includes all of the necessary elements we need for life. I think about how God has made the universe to be exactly so, so that all the effects of time and mass and light and motion held together by God has given us this precious place. My wondering is not unlike a child's with that wide-eyed abandoned interest in what was, what is, and what will be. I scarce can take it in. Some of what is is so much more than imaginable let alone all there is. God's touch is so amazing and so sure and we (how can I even dare) are made in his image. He has given to us those same attributes and such a strong design and desire to create. Let us be more like Him.

Grand Canyon

It is not a wonder to me the Grand Canyon so vast so wide but what was there before

Amazed I am to think of time gone by that washed the

Earth aside that moved the mountains to the shore

To look now deep and long across the river swift and strong

Most people think an awesome sight

I wonder where it all has gone

Up and down the canyon walls are spaces now where rock belonged.

Where plant and bird have left so long.

Yes there is a river at its' base some fish and creatures live in grace

But looking down the canyon length, unending foot of cubic space.

My wife and I were driving through the mountains in east Tennessee and the sun was setting in a distant valley. The clouds had settled in and the valley and it had the appearance of the mouth of a vast volcano. The sun began to set and was dropping behind the clouds. It was to take on the appearance of a fire with all the colors related to it, reds and oranges and white and blues and purples. This was so spectacular to us. We had quite a discussion on the awesomeness of the things of nature and how the creative affects of the natural surroundings were so unique and unmatched by anything man could do.

The clouds and sun mixed it up and the lower the sun set into the backdrop of the clouds the brighter and the fiercer it looked. You could actually see the clouds boil in the valley as a cauldron of fire. I wanted to be able to capture this picture but we had no way to photograph the event. This would have taken a lot more than I was able to film with the 35mm camera we had. We had to just settle for the memory of it and it was my hope to be able to express the picture in words. As the sun set the fiery appearance began to fade and then the night set in. That visual stays with us.

Sunset Behind the Clouds

Between the mountain tops and in the valley below

A glow of fire begins to show

More intense, as the moments leave behind

A brighter red with orange and white entwined

From way down low to a greater height

The billowing flame like clouds; ignite

Fire and smoke increase therein

Daylight fades as night sets in

Driving through the boot heel of Missouri at the end of winter. It was early in the morning and the sun was just beginning to rise. There was an ice storm the night before and there was ice everywhere. Ice in the fields, on the trees, on the bushes, on the roofs and on the roads. We had to drive carefully to keep from sliding off the road. It did seem the roads had sufficient warmth that the ice was melting off them first and made the driving easier as we moved on through the countryside. As I looked around the sight reminded me of an old black and white movie I saw when I was much younger. The movie was an adaptation of A Midsummer Nights Dream. I remember Mickey Rooney was very young and he played Puc and Victor Jory played some sort of evil character. In this fantasy fairy tail styled movie there was a lot of sparkling lights and stars and flashing of reflective fairy dust. The ice on the grasses in the field froze the grasses in the upright position where I might have thought just the sheer weight of the ice would crush it down but it didn't. Ice coated all the leaves and limbs in the trees and bushes. The ponds where the livestock drank were partially frozen over and around the banks on one side or the other was something akin to steam rising and moving across the field and dissipating into the sky. I have thought for years on this scene and wondered if it would be even possible for me to describe how it looked in my mind. I do not think I could have captured a picture, which would show the dimension of interest that had captured my imagination.

Diamonds

Looking into the distance in the early morn

Icy and cold from the freezing storm,

The sun rising, shining across the vault

With radiant rays' dancing in the fields

Shards of ice every size and shape reflecting light

Moving through meadowland and mountain roads

Each shard catching a glint and tossing it unrestrained

A flash of light strikes the eye

Then jumps from shard to shard glistening like Diamonds

Earth folding in toward the sun bringing warmth

Soon as sun begins to rise the Diamonds melt before our eyes.

How sad to see that vision go sinking into earth below.

Memories are refreshing to the soul and as our mind with eyes closed captures the essence of a moment in time it refreshes our life if only for that moment.

Morning Time

Stepping out into the morning air

There is a feel and a smell not unfamiliar.

Dampness to my skin

With perspiration beginning to bead droplets

A cloud overhead with small bursts of energy

A drop of rain or two hits the dry ground

Forcing small puffs of dust upward

Into my nostrils an earthy odor

One that brings an emotion so deep it is not understood

Thinking on that the rain builds

The mist of water fills the air

And washes the perspiration from my arms

Memories of time gone by fill my mind and soul

A cleansing peace then comes over me.

Waking to a storm can actually bring a kind of feeling of security. I do not know exactly what it is but it make us feel warm and in want of a certain kind of comfort. Seeing a storm move its way through gives bit of an insight to life itself. Some things batter us and pour down on us and then it begins to let up and we finally see the light and in doing so we feel a release and a rest and we raise our hands and voices to the Lord for preserving us. I think there is such a picture of Gods cleansing in a rainstorm.

Weather

I awoke with the sound of thunder rolling through the atmosphere

Rain misting across the yards and neighborhoods

Heavier came the rain till torrents of water rushed down the street

Drops of rain hitting flowers with violence bending petals and stems

Weighing down leaves and limbs breaking down the deadwood,

   crashing to the ground

The rain slowing back to a mist gently washing the faces of the flowers

Seeing the sun peak through, closed flowers open to the welcome warmth

Leaves and limbs and plant stems rising toward the sun as in worship

We often get bogged down with the minutia of life and so many trappings get in our way that to get past them takes a concentrated effort to place ourselves where we can be successful in our focus on God. It then is time to recognize we need to use all we are and have available and keep moving not on how we feel but what the truth is. To quote "it is the voice of truth that tells a different story". This truth points to the one we need to trust. The enemy will rob us in so many ways and of so much if we let him, our existence will be in jeopardy. God will not leave us behind and will not forsake us. He will never allow a bruised reed to be broken.

Trust

When thinking about nature of things

How it all works and what it all brings

So much time is wasted on non-essentials

Head to head with life's potentials

Makes more sense to forge ahead

With all your might and without dread

Trusting your heart and soul and mind

to the one who will never leave you behind.

Life Struggles

A man said to me that Hope to him was like crack cocaine you keep right on reaching back to it for more and you cannot let it go. You will do so much to see that hope is fulfilled in your life and that includes being patient for very long periods of time. Hope deferred makes a heart grow sick but when it comes; it is a tree of life.

Born into Darkness

Born into darkness with the struggle to move into light

Looking in every direction for a hope

Some small sign, some little light, a glimpse of future

Maybe only one or two minutes or a tangible sight

Over there; move toward that, a passing brightness

Attempting to grasp only to have it slip away

Another twinkle and again it slips by without a chance

Hope being ever illuminating and more revolutionary

Never giving up or giving in, finally seeing, grasping

Growing into the radiance of the emanation of life

An ebullient personification of who we were meant to be

It is in the struggles of our lives we can become stronger. By looking to God for strength because He is the way out of our trouble. In our trouble God supports us and lifts us from the struggles while holding us in the place we need to be.

The Mire

You cannot grow without the mire of life

Your strength increased while walking through strife

While sinking deeper seems hope disappears

Deep waters rush over and our vision blurs

We cry out for the lifter of our head

But you oh Lord are the lifter of my head

Nothing more I want than to be in your Grace

As you lift my head to feel the sweetness of your embrace

Pull me up into the son light and kiss my face

Have you been in a place where the expectations of your life by others have been more than you could bear? They want you to be something you are not to make themselves feel more comfortable. So they set about to change you by suggesting the various things you need to do to be a better person while they do not seek to change their own heart.

Pressed to Change

I want to write about my heart

I want to sing, there is no song

A box so small with pressure great

Was placed in my heart to sit and wait

A ball was found to place in my heart

To round the corners from the box

My heart was pressed and pulled and stretched

To mold me what was thought was best

Ridged now my heart to change

A balm I need to heal my pain

Life is fraught with all kinds of tough issues and to every tough issue there is an answer.

Life

Sufficient in mistakes

Cloaked with personal aches

Sufficient in errors

Suffocating with mental terrors

Sufficient in sorrow

Nothing of time to borrow

Forgiveness quakes

More powerful than mistakes

Mercy, God the bearer

Shielder of the terror

Love is given, not to borrow

Fortified from our sorrow

I honestly find it hard to speak of this and how this came to me. I had gone through some very difficult times and as it is when you go through some things in life it is not just you who is to suffer. I was the cause of many around me to suffer and take pause in their life. It seemed unredeemable to me and even to some others. I will say I stood up, took what was coming to me and I expected much more than I received. I am here to say God is the one hundred percent redeemer. After a time I was having a conversation with an acquaintance who had been around during that time. We began to talk about the plate we are served and how difficult it is to eat all we are served. He said I have seen you eat your plate clean. Eating all you were served and there is redemption not for the works of it but for the willingness. I am grateful to God for his preservation and His redemption in my life and my family and those around me I so negatively affected. I have seen some hang on to their grievance of that time and not forgive me. Fortunately that is not for me to deal with.

The plate you are served

I have been served a plate

Bitter, sweet, savory, bland, and fat

Looking at it I said I couldn't eat all that

All of this is for your betterment

Eating all is a personal testament

Beginning to eat; I found; the bigger it looked

Some fresh and raw some cold some cooked

Sometimes overwhelmed as day by day

Eating what was on my plate was good

Sometimes hard so I would pray

Some would mix which seemed much worse

Some that mixed seemed much like a curse

I have seen this plate served to all around

They picked and chose what they would eat

Lacking strength to pass life's feats

They faulted; halted; and then they stopped

I said; I've eaten all that is on my plate

Now I've been asked to drink of the cup

Resolution

There is a tremendous struggle in our minds when we even consider the aspects of laying our lives before God. It is the unknown. Our experience with God through our time spent shows us His undeniable care for us and gives us a comfort to let Him have control in our walk with Him.

Surrender

Complete and total surrender

That is what I am here after

Not to give in to self or claim my life

Here to say I take it all and not by the knife

But by the Sword of truth and not of my might

Laying it down, letting God sort my plight

I think a lot about hope. It almost appears to me that hope is an entity in itself. I think it has a life of its own and is demonstrated in the basic premises of possibilities. The very point of disconnecting someone from hope removes his or her life. Literally it removes the ability to move forward in any positive way. A man of great hope sees all the possibilities even in distressing times. He can see there is a future and if he can just make it through this next moment he will be ok. A man with no hope will not only end his future but has no compunction to end the future of all those around him. It is difficult to present hope to a man who has no hope; so it could be the presentation that of his last and his first hope is Jesus.

Hope

Hope in our present state of life

Brings to us the possibilities of each tomorrow

An expectation of things to come

A grasping of all that is at our hand

The touch of joy and sovereign grace

If hope is gone the distant fields only linger

As a wisp of smoke disappears in the atmosphere

Holding to hope with all our strength

Is as an incense ever before Gods face

Out in your world there are people who are in need of real encouragement. Sometime in your life it is quite possible you have been through something similar so you begin to share that particular place of your experience in hopes it will lift them even a little. There comes a response back from them you could not have expected. Some may say you really don't have that right or you can't imagine where I am in this pain and with all your understanding you cannot see why you were rejected in your approach to encourage. You wore your heart in the open as you were baring your soul just to bring a spark of life to them.

Giving Hope

I sought to show the world my heart

Some looked and mused upon my pain

Few really cared what I shared

Some said; if you only knew what I've been through

To show my heart was not to say

I've been through more than you today

But just to give a ray of hope

It is simply taking a hard look at who you are and not being the man who takes a look in the mirror and when he turns away forgets what he looks like. Taking a hard look and making a decision that you serve something or someone is very important in your life. Not making a decision is a decision.

It is your nature

A user, a schemer, a profit, a teacher

Abuser, deceiver, or a soul-searching seeker

Embattled, embittered, run over by strife

A time must come to bring you to life

Do not overlook what you have lived

But look to what you are to become

The who you were should not be your sum

Like the scorpion and snake or beast on the run

Stop what you're doing and turn to the One

Who's in control; you, the devil, or Son

Feeling alone moving through our day to day can be as Moses when he was on the back side of the desert living his life waiting for what. It may be he did not know or though because of his mistakes he was all through with his portion of Gods purposes for him. I think we can be so surprised by what God has in store for us.

Manna

Taking a tour of the backside of the desert.

I feel like I have been walking here a long time

Quite desperate for any answer no desire to be inert

Moving slowly as an old Kine much to benign

I am waiting for my (what is this?)

Something never had nor seen before

I anticipate while waiting to see the things in store

When walking through the open door

God

I have a strong sense of what it is to live a life off the beaten path and away from the calling I have been given. I have lived there and suffered there.

A Moment

To think of spending a moment without you

I cannot think of that, nor could it be true

My mind may stray and my life may go awry

My heart may fade and my spirit may dry

Thinking of this one thing I know is true

Never spending a moment without you

There is a song, which says; Where do I go when there is no foundation stable? Where do I go when the storms of life assail? I go to the rock of my salvation.

My Refuge

Can it be in the pain of life and love there is no place to go?

When all has slipped away and it seems no one to hold.

How can it be the suffering of my soul has joined to one so dear?

There is no other place than the hand of God so near.

For he is my refuge and my hiding place so clear.

Nothing can be said of God that has not already been spoken but we keep trying, don't we?

To Speak of God

Writing this song about God, I can think of no ground that has not been covered

To speak of love and Grace or what is my place around all these words I hovered

To sing of his mercy, which lasts forever, His care for all is like no other

To speak eternally of things remembered, promises fulfilled could never be penned

The words we know will not describe the fullness of whom we shall never transcend

I was thinking how the Father has come to me so many times in my meditation and alone times. I hear his voice in a sweet whisper small and still, comforting. He has let me know He was with me in my joy and in my sorrow. That He was the lifter of my head and my strength. How often I forget that and have to be called back to his protection. It speaks to me of my willfulness and my independent spirit. You know the one that leads you into trouble and you just follow like you are mindless. God woos my spirit back to him in such a sweet way. God is my salvation and my strength.

Whispers

In listening to the sweet whispers of God

Is he saying I have seen the places you have trod

Have you heard him whisper how he loves you

And with tenderness he speaks your spirit I will woo

He lifts your head so you can see his face

In doing so you are lifted up in grace

I was sitting in a restaurant one day and some fellows about two tables from me were having a conversation about life and jobs and politics. In there conversation they swore quite a bit and it was bothersome to me. They were pretty loud. I thought on what they said and every so often they said Jesus or Jesus Christ. I recognized how grateful I was for that name.

Your Name

I listened as they talked of love today

Of peace and joy and hope

In their words I heard your name

With profane text I heard your name

They used your name with love and joy

It did not bring them peace

And hope was left so far behind

Yet in your name today I find

To me it spoke of peace and joy

and love and hope in kind

Prophetic

There is an expectation of our tomorrows, even though we realize we cannot predict anything that will happen. Sometimes being honest in our hearts and praying exactly how we feel is the best thing to do.

Prayer for The Day

I do not know how to pray today

I know I am not satisfied in my work or play

A little angry not seeing clearly

A little empty hoping sincerely

I tend to stray without results

I feel vulnerable to the enemy's assaults

Help me to see my way through today

Be my help and strength; this is what I pray.

The last few years we have heard the word of the later rain and the Spirit of God raining in our time and recently I have heard so much more about God raining and refreshing us, and the pouring out of His Spirit on all mankind. In the last few months I have heard about it from many sources and even on face book one of my friends quoted a scripture related to the Spirit of God raining his presence. I believe this is what God placed in my heart about the subject of the rain of the Spirit.

Rain

I pray for Rain.

Of course it is the sunshine that strengthens and gives focus.

Rain can be doleful and perhaps a little delicate.

Rain makes things indistinct and rain makes us slow down.

Rain also cleans the air and moves stain and silt to lower ground.

Let it rain and move me to higher ground.

Rain strengthens the root to make the plant stronger.

Of course the sunshine strengthens and gives focus.

Without the rain our soul would dry.

Rain on my face, running down my neck, feels cleansing and redemptive,

Bringing my senses to life, while trails of rain drip from arms and fingertips.

Washing the day from hair and skin running to the ground,

Moving down street, and walk, through the grass to lower ground.

Oh let it rain and let me stand on higher ground.

Of course it is the Son that gives strength and focus.

So I pray for rain.

I raise my hands to receive the rain

One drop then another and another

Drizzling then pouring

Open arms reaching, stretching to receive

Knowing it is the Son that brings the Rain.

Looking straight into the sky

Rain anointing my head, running into my eyes

Filling my mouth with clear cool water

Wanting for more, I am not filled yet

Receiving more, refreshing myself

Knowing this, it is the Son that brings the Rain.

The clouds pouring down more and more

Emptying on dry ground renewing the parched

and dry land

Refreshing land and people

With all goodness and prosperity and strengthening them

In Newness and Spirit and Knowledge and Fruitfulness.

So I pray for Rain.

I often question why I keep doing what I am doing because I see no results. Face it we are result oriented people. We will settle for second or third best if we have to wait to long. Our lives consist of sowing seeds. We sow seeds of all types and varieties. We are impatient and in a hurry for the things we sow to come to maturity.
Listening to the voice of God in where and how we sow is significant to our destinies. Being patient and being filled with Hope to see the fruit of what we have sown is holding us to the hope of that very destiny.

Sowing Seed

I looked out into the field and saw it was dry and parched

I was told to plow the fallow ground hard and scorched

Why would I do that my heart did respond

Nothing would grow in the thirsty barren place

Now I should cast the seed I heard the voice resound

No fertile soil I saw so why should I sow a seed

I am sure it will not grow

No rain in sight, with passing time and no produce.

Why would I keep this up with no fruit in sight you might deduce?

I was obedient to what I was told even though I knew

Nothing would grow with the seed I sowed

I am so sure not one thing would grow; yet obedient

In the distance rumblings are heard

A cloud I see and I know it's being true; that word

In examining all I am sure it was Gods voice that I heard

In it's nature let the earth rebound with all its might

Let the earth rebound and my spirit soar.

Gods word is true whether we have one or nothing in sight.

Several years ago I was on a motorcycle trip with some friends from church. We were on the Blue Ridge Park Way and The Cheeriola Parkway in North Carolina. We arrived on a Friday night and I roomed with a gentleman my wife and I met on an earlier trip. We engaged in a conversation of jobs and life and heart desires and a number of other things to pass the time. I recently saw the movie Tombstone. I gave him my take on the essence of Wyatt Earp and I do take a little license here when I give my personal thoughts on Wyatt. I believe God has moved on certain people throughout history to take a particular stand against evil and sometimes even in there lack of understanding of why they have such a drive or bend toward righteousness. I believe Wyatt Earp was placed where he was to do a job for a time in a place that no one else had the wherewithal to accomplish. He stood up against those who were destroying the lives of communities' for there own benefit. He stepped in but not by himself. He developed relationships with people who were able to be a support to him in one way or another, and it was his will and his fire that drove them. There are many examples of men throughout history who had great influence on small communities and large alike.

We slept the night and were refreshed in the morning when we began our bike trip. The lead man seemed to be taking the turns in the road at a relatively fast pace and some of the other bikers were not as experienced so they went a bit slower and soon the lead with some more experienced bikers moved on out of sight. The man right in front of me was making a turn and hit a small grassy area and his bike wobbled and flipped him off and under the bike and he slid about a hundred plus feet hitting his head on a curb with such force he bounced, literally folded in half and then came to rest with the bike on top of him. When I came upon him his eyes were completely glazed over and not breathing and for a moment I was sure he was dead. Breath suddenly came to him and his eyes began to clear up. That moment for me was almost a relief until I realized I was all by myself and now I would have to take care of him and help him. He asked me to move the bike off him. I first told him that I realized he may be in a lot of pain but he needed to take stock of his body from head to toe before I moved anything. The motorcycle had a rigged pedal and the place where the pedal was, was directly over his stomach. If that was penetrating him in any way and I pulled it off. Well I will leave that to your imagination. I then removed the bike and administered first aid to him. Help came and we moved him to a hospital. His wounds were redressed and he spent the rest of the trip in his hotel room taking pain meds.

So here I was telling the story of God placing a man in a place for a purpose. I did not realize that man for this time and this place would be me. I was told later there was no one on this trip that had a clue about what to do but me. How interesting.

A Man

There is a man set up in a place and time
To deal the righteousness of God sublime
To clear the way for the peace in that place
Unerring, relentless, regretless, and base
Who is solid and upright to discharge the case
Giving himself to a particular cause
Set to the task with not even a pause

I had a dream one night and saw a huge perfectly formed tree in the center of a field. At least to my mind it was perfect. There was a breeze blowing and a river flowing around the tree. The water was clear and teaming with life. There was fruit on the tree and many people desired the fruit. The waters were bubbling the way I remember artesian wells bubbling to the surface.

I worked in the great cypress swamp in 1969 in Florida, which is on the edge of the everglades. I worked on a surveying team and we were in the thick of the swamp all day every day. A couple of times I remember running into one of those types of water flows coming from under the ground and bursting up and bubbling with clear fresh water. It was pretty amazing to see. Small fish and creatures would swim in and out and around it seemingly to celebrate it. Watching it gave me a sense of the potential of new life full of joy and hope.

Tree

In the center of it all the tree of life still stands

As the tree planted by the waters

Forever rooted in the eternal truth and word of life

The ever flowing river with all its' spiritual depth and width

Nurturing everything and every being

Continual renewal bubbling forth from its' refreshing waters.

Healing all who come to its' fountain for forgiveness and health.

For spiritual strength, knowledge, wisdom and understanding.

Haiti First Trip

This is the first trip I made to Haiti. The trip came six months after the earthquake and actually it was not less than I expected because of the news and research I did before the trip. I went with a group from our church and in the group was a good mix of ages and skills for our effort. When we arrived we were picked up at the airport and taken to a church compound and school where we were to stay for the following week. We were on a second and third floor of the building and we slept on concrete floors. If you were properly prepared it was still quite a challenge to sleep and function in any way that seemed normal. There were two bathrooms with three or four showers each and one toilet for some thirty plus people.

Each one of us suffered some ills throughout the week some much worse than others but it did give us a taste of life in Haiti on a personal level. These are some insights I had during the time of this first trip. This first trip is engraved in my memory as though it were tattooed on my heart. Each moment, each step, each feeling, smell and sound

Our first full day was involved in the services at the property we stayed and it was actually pretty amazing. The people came from all around the city. Lest I forget we were in (Port O Prince) in one of the more populated areas. When the people came to church they were dressed to the Nines clean and all pressed with the best they had. It was amazing to see them especially knowing where they had to come from and just how incredibly hot and dusty it was.

Who Me

We entered the church and were ushered to a specific place

I know we were guests but this for me took a particular grace

In seeing this building fill up face after face place after place

Looking sharp and pressed and clean and me in my jeans

Wearing my pullover shirt with wrinkles and stretched out seams

Knowing where this great number of people stayed the night before

Gave me pause in thinking who I was and what was in store

From six am till nine pm giving themselves to worship and adore

The Lord of all of us who brought us together at this time and place

In my eyes it was they who should have had that seat of grace

And me that should have been able to lift them in a Godly embrace

Services started at 6:30 am and they had classes and teaching and more services until late at night. All I can say is; how awesome is our God.

Our first day of work and being back at the compound was so tiring and exhausting and the days that followed became even harder. I would not trade this experience for anything.

End of the day

Riding back from the jobs on the wooden and tin bus

Gave me pause to think of what awaited all of us

A time of rest and reflection and a calculation

How would we fit our showers in the men and the women

Who would be first then second or last

Someone would hurry and some would get passed

Did each one watch out for the next one who needed

Or did by chance we fit in by how shower space conceded

Relinquishing itself to the next and the next

However there always seemed to be some order to the way

So grateful we were for the all the provisions of the day

A couple days arriving at the school from our jobsite

Folks endeavored to rebuild till late at night

Rain moved in with a refreshing breeze

Not long lived but pretty sweet by degrees

Then time for bed and a long night of the dogs

Barking all hours, not intimidated they slogged

Sleep barely fogging our eyes it was time to start over again

As the time went by I wondered about the landscape and the lack of animals other than the domesticated ones we saw pretty regularly. It was so conspicuous by the absence of wild life I could not help but wonder.

On a further trip to a different ministry I was discussing the thoughts of the lack of wildlife with one of the property managers and why it may be so sparse; without a pause when I asked he said and with no provocation "they must have all been eaten". I wrote this months before I had this moment with him.

Haitian wild life

I thought I heard mosquitoes would be everywhere

I saw one maybe two or three or four

More flies than anything and they were everywhere

Only one sparrow not Jack Sparrow the pirate

Just the bird

Four blackbirds not in a pie just flying in the sky

Five seabirds of one kind or another

Where are the seagulls I asked and no one knew

One snake on the ground but butterflies did abound

One cat or maybe two; lots of goats walking through

Cattle here and there; a flock of sheep or two

I saw no or wasps or bees even looking to the trees

You'd expect to see bees near trees or in flowers close by

I saw some dogs but they all looked the same and it gave me cause to wonder

Is the wild life in the mountains high above the cityscapes?

Hiding out of sight away to keep them safe

(Or have they all been eaten.)

This is only a thought I had about the showers.

Showers

I thought each night how nice to be able to take a shower.
Stepping in and turning on the water having second thoughts
As the cool water hit my head and then
trickling down my back to the floor it took my breath away.
Yet it felt so refreshing and good. Standing still while giving
in to the sensation of the cold and not being able to think while
my body adjusted to the temperature of the water I gradually
began to catch my breath and relax under the trickle from the
garden style faucet. It was very nice to have that luxury in a
place like that. I saw many people washing themselves out in
the street and everyone could see, with no privacy or attempt to hide.
For me the showers were like a ride at the fair when the flume
hits the water and it buries you with a big wave.
Not a minute or two after drying off it seemed as though
I never even stepped in the shower. Hot and sweaty, still.

Although there were many people in the throws of daily life there seemed to be quiet over the people. There was noise and conversation but not an energy you might expect in normal conditions.

Silence

God is good no matter what the condition

He is God what ever your philosophical position

Words crafted by our lips, erased by what we do

Not always said but done shows what is true

In the depth of despair the people are screaming out

In silence, louder than any spoken word or shout

Deep unto deep the pleading

Strength depleted with no leading

No satisfaction replete with sorrow

God is good even though you are fallow

He is God and hears the sound of your silence

Each silence or sorrow, are soothed by His presence

This is my attempt to paint a picture for you of moving through the city.

The City

Climbing onto the bus in the early morning

Sleep still in our eyes the day ahead of us

Thinking and plotting then planning

What lies ahead; will it build or crush

Jerking, jolting with each bump in the road

Counting each time my head hit the ceiling

Or crashing against the side trying to avoid protrusions

Metal and bolts and steel rails with sharp edges

Grasping, holding with all my might not to be frapped

As in a giant blender with all the ingredients, its fruits and juices

In with the mix, the noises from the streets

Voices heard above the sound of the bus

Honking and beeping horns of every pitch and sound

The smells boiling, steaming upward, filling our noses

Like sledge hammers against our senses they pound

When will we be through this or away a question poses

Braking and starting then braking again

Watching through cutout windows the people at the ground

Beautiful faces, all made by the hand of God

All looking for something to satisfy

A little money or a touch or kind word a moment to be alone

Something, anything to bring a little hope to help them through the day

Everyone moving and focused all about the day's business

All we have today is what we will give

Our energy, a little of this, a little of that

But most affective is our love and prayers

First impression replaced by fact.

The Haiti Worship Team

At first look our group seemed to be all about the fun

Not all but some

A few here and a few there joked and laughed

As the time went by you could see much deeper

And from time to time the talk and laughter turned to the Son

Nothing wrong with giggles and grins

Joking and laughing are definitely not sins

Each conversation throughout the week was filled with worship

Lifting up the name of Jesus, how He loves us, and how He sees us

Careful thought in each and every word and statement

Careful crafting to me just showed how reverent

Each one vulnerable and open to each other

To share the Son with each sister and brother

Worship is to whisper His name to each other.

At the end of our time in Haiti we went to a restaurant in the mountains and I sat with some ladies. One of the ladies and myself had a discussion of the work we did but at the forefront was the sheer amount of energy it took us to get to the job site. We had to walk through what to us seemed like swamp and a comment was made that it actually seemed like another planet we were trekking. No pun intended. We had to carry all of our water and tools for each day and move through water and walk on rocks slipping and calculating each step. By the time we reached or destination we were already exhausted except for a few hardy folks. Everyone on our team had at least one day where they could not function and again except for a few hardy individuals.

As we were in discussion about the trip one person and including myself became very emotional about the difficulty of this way we were in. Thinking about one more trip to the job was so much more than could be borne in our hearts.

One step

Just the thought of walking that path one more time

Steppingstones placed to keep you dry

One step after another, after another, after another

Carefully placing your feet so not to slip in the slime

Thirty minutes may be forty-five one more time we have to try

Trying will not do, thinking of each sister and brother

Who walk this way every day, one day, one step at a time.